DOORS OF LEARNING
MICROCOSMS OF A FUTURE
SOUTH AFRICA

T0016217

SPECTOR BOOKS

CONTENTS

Doors of Learning
Microcosms of a Future
South Africa

Bauhaus Lab 2022

The archives of the Bauhaus Dessau Foundation house an extensive collection of documents about the two Habitat seminars which were organised by the Bauakademie der DDR (Architectural Academy of the GDR) at what was then known as the Zentrum für Gestaltung Bauhaus Dessau (Bauhaus Dessau Centre of Design). The first seminar in 1987 involving international experts took place as part of the UN's International Year of Shelter for the Homeless and had the somewhat unwieldy title 'Experience of the GDR in solving the housing problem and its relevance for developing countries'. The list of participants includes architects and planners from Angola, Ghana, Iraq, Ethiopia, Egypt, Syria, Tanzania, Kenya, Zimbabwe and from the African National Congress (ANC). A second event was held a year later — a seminar at which a prefabricated building system was introduced. It had been developed by GDR architects at the Institute for Urban Planning and Architecture (ISA) of the Bauakademie and was implemented at the ANC's Dakawa Development Centre.[1]

The documents held by the Bauhaus Dessau Foundation shed little light on the Habitat seminar. More information is found in an article in a 1989 issue of the magazine *Architektur der DDR* (Architecture of the GDR), in which the architect Peter Wurbs, who was personally involved in the project, reports on the project in some depth. Under the aegis of the UN Habitat programme, the ANC and the Solidarity Committee of the GDR had decided on a joint project to introduce the WPC (wall panel column) method in the ANC's Dakawa Development Centre. This centre helped the ANC provide education and a home for young South Africans fleeing the apartheid regime. Dakawa, like the nearby Solomon Mahlangu Freedom College (SOMAFCO), was not only a testing ground which sought to build up a new society that did away with the phantom of racial segregation but also an example of transnational cooperation between East and West during the Cold War in the name of international solidarity and the anti-apartheid movement, which had support worldwide.

The project launched in 1987 envisaged the construction of a mobile prefabrication unit as well as training for ANC teams taking place in Bautzen, East Germany. Together with brigades from the Freie Deutsche Jugend (FDJ, official youth organisation in the GDR), these teams would then build day care centres and other planned housing types on location in Tanzania. The project also was to provide on-site training for what the article calls 'unskilled labourers'.[2]

The Bauakademie's documents are held in the archive of the Leibnitz Institute for Research on Society and Space (IRS), where more traces of the Dakawa project are found. In the correspondence between the Central Council of the FDJ, the ISA of the Bauakademie, the East German government's Solidarity Committee and the Building Ministry, the difficulties of implementing the project are discussed. These include the deficiencies of prefabricated building components and the resulting expense of subsequent works, the lack of technical skills among the FDJ builders and local labourers, infestation with termites, etc.[3]

The reports indicate a sense of urgency and emphasise how very important this project is for the international recognition of the GDR.

This significance was likewise highlighted in the article in the magazine *Architektur der DDR,* in which it is stated: 'With the productive prefabrication plant and the structural completion of the kindergarten, a convincing reference object for the efficiency of the WPC method has been realised in Central Africa. For the GDR, this constitutes an internationally noteworthy contribution to the International Year of Shelter for the Homeless (IYSH).'[4]

Why was this project ascribed such political importance in the GDR at a time in which the standardised industrialised construction technologies used to help solve the housing shortage in what were then called Third World countries were already the subject of intense international criticism? Since the mid-1970s, international architects had turned against low-cost housing development strategies and espoused projects orientated towards local building traditions, materials and practices. Habitat I, the first United Nations Conference on Human Settlements, held in 1976 in Vancouver, called for an understanding of 'housing as a basic human right and as a practice of communal creation' and thus set in motion a paradigm shift in development policy. This moved away from the standardised, highly technical one-size-fits-all solutions influenced by Western actors such as the IMF, the World Bank and the UN, which had not resolved poverty and homelessness, but had instead helped create new dependencies worldwide. A document found in the ANC Archives at the University of Fort Hare reflects the tenor of this criticism. Here, the master plan for the Dakawa education centre proposed by the Norwegian company Norplan is discussed from precisely that perspective of stepping away from the modernistic development aid paradigm. The report asks: 'Are they planning a mini-Brasília?' The criticism focused on the sanitary installations, designed to meet Western standards despite an acute water shortage in the region, as well as on the building materials and technologies, the question being why local building materials and methods were not used here.[5]

The GDR's engagement in Dakawa must be seen in the context of the active attempts to achieve international recognition from the 1970s onwards, which had reached a new stage after the Hallstein Doctrine was abandoned and found expression in membership of the UN. On an international level, in various organisations, conferences and projects, architecture and housing development became fields of interaction and exchange between Eastern and Western Bloc powers and postcolonial nations. But pragmatic economic motivations, such as the access to urgently needed Western currencies, made the Dakawa project a highly political affair too.

At the same time, this argument falls short if it does not move beyond the framework of the system of comparison between East and West, which sees the GDR's engagement in Dakawa merely as proof of the battle for international recognition. In fact, the confluence of Norwegian, Finnish, East German,

Tanzanian, Danish and South African actors in Dakawa is a manifestation of a development that has long been disregarded in the historiography of globalisation. Contemporary historians rightly criticise the way in which the role of socialist and postcolonial nations is omitted from the historiography of global 20th century interrelations, which describe the West as the sole driver of such interconnections and treat the 'rest' as isolated and excluded from these.[6] How socialist projects around the world were interconnected economically, politically and culturally, which processes and collaborations alternative models of international trade reproduced and how global geographies changed in the wake of anticolonial liberation movements are also all questions that the Bauhaus Lab 2022 grappled with. Ultimately, the two ANC development centres were places in which the plurality of different forms of internationalism coincided, with all the resultant tensions, controversies and conflicts.

This publication is a result of the research, debates, meetings and excursions as well as the jointly organised exhibition realised by the eight international participants of the Bauhaus Lab 2022. They describe these settlements as hubs for transnational networks comprising aid organisations, groups of actors, material flows, knowledge transfers, technologies, educational agendas and diverse political interests. At the same time, they portray these centres as concrete lived-in places and realms offering experiences of 'international solidarity' which live on in the life stories of their former inhabitants.

Regina Bittner

Networks of international solidarity

ANTI-COLONIAL EDUCATION AND SOLIDARITY IN THE ANC EXILE CENTRES

The Bauhaus Lab's 2022 edition approached the broad topic of international anti-apartheid solidarity movements, delving into the understudied history of two educational centres located in Tanzania, more than 2,500 kilometres away from South Africa. They were founded by the African National Congress (ANC) to accommodate and educate children, teenagers and young adults who had to flee the South African apartheid regime's oppression and persecution during the 1970s and 1980s.

Nelson Mandela's party, the aforementioned ANC, was banned as an illegal organisation in South Africa in 1960. From then on, it had to operate from abroad[1] and shifted its strategy from passive to armed resistance.

A major humanitarian crisis began in 1976, when an uprising against racially dividing education, which today is known as the Soweto Uprising, was met with fierce police brutality, shootings, killings and persecution. Those who survived were in an extremely vulnerable position and needed protection. As an emergency measure arranged by the ANC, children were sent to Dar es Salaam, Tanzania. The ANC and Tanzania's ruling party Chama Cha Mapinduzi (CCM) by then maintained a very good relationship. Furthermore, Tanzania was already providing facilities for a number of African liberation movements, allowing them to operate from its soil since 1962. Yet, for the young and traumatised South Africans there wasn't any ideal infrastructure immediately available. The Solomon Mahlangu Freedom College (SOMAFCO) and the Dakawa Development Centre were built in response to the shelter problem they faced on arrival in Tanzania. The intertwined history of these centres has to be regarded as part of a bigger framework instead of only pertaining to South Africa's or Tanzania's history. They constitute a chapter in the history of organised resistances of African liberation movements, thus, necessarily, they should be seen in the broader context of Pan-Africanism. An ambitious political project, Pan-Africanism may be summarised as the quest for African unity and cooperation beyond ethnic divisions and exploitation. It was an ideology shared by the most prominent leaders of African liberation movements.

Research on the ground was essential in order to arrive at relevant findings, thus, the Bauhaus Lab team formed two groups: One travelled to South Africa with the purpose of consulting specific archives, and another was responsible of surveying the actual sites. Drawing on findings from both and also on secondary sources, this article intends to place these two ANC resistance centres in the history of Pan-Africanism and its efforts for African liberation and self-determination, highlighting the centres' commitment to Pan-African anti-colonial education. In the conclusion, we shall raise some questions about the 'ambiguities' of international solidarity in the Cold War context.

The increasing number of African states becoming independent from 1960 onwards was an important backdrop for the ANC after its ban from South Africa since many of these freshly liberated countries were concerned with a Pan-African agenda and actively committed to Africa's liberation from colonial rule and apartheid.[2]

● Sam Nujoma, Julius Nyerere and Oliver Tambo at a Frontline States meeting in Dar es Salaam

Within this context, Julius Nyerere, Tanzania's first president, was a central figure in the Pan-African drive for independence. He strongly believed that Tanzania had a responsibility to actively assist other African nations in achieving freedom from foreign and minority rule and had an important role in supporting the ANC in its forced exile from South Africa. For example, Tanzania allowed freedom fighters to live and train in military camps especially conceived for African liberation movements (for instance in the understudied camps formerly located in the cities of Kongwa, Morogoro, Mbeya and Bagamoyo).

Given the influx of people and the subsequent shelter crisis triggered by the Soweto Uprising, Dar es Salaam started to be overcrowded. Yet, there was a much more serious problem: It was potentially dangerous for South African exiles to be in Dar es Salaam, considering that pro-apartheid spies and mercenaries could be on their trail.[3] Therefore, aware of this security issue, the Tanzanian administration decided to move them to the Morogoro region. Provisionally, they were moved to Mzinga, near a military camp,[4] until in early 1977 they were offered a strategically chosen area in Mazimbu, 10 kilometres from the city of Morogoro, where the ANC would establish an educational centre.[5] Local politician Annah Abdallah[6] played an important role as intermediary, strongly sympathising with the project and giving constant support.

● Finnish-made Kutter school bus donated to the ANC by the Association of Finnish Adult Education Organisation

● Oliver Tambo (right) arriving with Amílcar Cabral (left) at the OAU Heads of State meeting in Algiers, 1968

Gradually evolving 'from bush to a modern complex,'[7] the Solomon Mahlangu Freedom College, as it was later named, received international assistance from several governments and organisations. In the words of ANC member and architect Spencer Hodgson, interviewed by our team, the centres were the result of 'perhaps the biggest ever international solidarity and mobilisation campaign in history'.[8] A great educational experiment started. SOMAFCO served as a laboratory where educational theories could be put to the test, not shying away from an openly revolutionary horizon.

An ANC document of 1978 stated that the school's objectives were (1) 'to prepare cadres to serve the national struggle of the people of South Africa in the phase of the struggle for seizure of political power and the post liberation phase' and (2) 'to produce such cadres as will be able to serve the society in all fields, i.e., political, economic, socio-cultural, educational and scientific'.[9]

To achieve these goals, the ANC drew heavily on an approach known as 'education with production'.[10] It also relied on the experience of other African liberation movements from countries like Namibia, Zambia, Zimbabwe and Guinea-Bissau,[11] which, each in their own ways, tried to implement concepts of equality and self-reliance in education initiatives. One could also argue there was a connection to Tanzania's 'education for self-reliance', a motto of Nyerere's *Ujamaa* concept,[12] though this is disputed by Brown Maaba, suggesting instead a fragile 'elective affinity'.[13]

SOMAFCO was a melting pot of teaching styles and pedagogies deriving, directly or indirectly, from the Soviet Union, East Germany, Sweden, the Netherlands and from Christian mission schools. Subjects studied by 1988 included: mathematics, English, geography, history, biology, chemistry, physics, agricultural science, integrated science, typing, technical drawing, literature, art, development of societies and history of the struggle. Development of societies was a Soviet-influenced analysis of world history, while history of the struggle, a compulsory subject, dealt with the movement for South African liberation, examining the relationship between the political and armed struggles and how SOMAFCO students were themselves a part of it. The underlying message was that the armed struggle was key to the revolution but must necessarily go hand in hand with the political struggle.[14]

Pre-primary children were taught revolutionary songs, and older students had their own newspaper, which published their own poetry 'on themes such as oppression, exploitation, poverty, white privilege and black suffering'.[15]

EDUCATION AS A FORM OF MULTINATIONAL RESISTANCE

Support from the international community came as donations of goods, funds and manpower channelled to educational facilities at the centres. Global solidarity programmes covered all levels of education from kindergarten and elementary school to vocational and adult education. Anti-apartheid movements in the Global North were often built on a sense of a shared struggle against oppressive forces, and many

● Workers at the garment workshop

anti-apartheid programmes demonstrated student-to-student or labour-to-labour motives.[16] Within the global development industry, education was seen as one of the most efficient forces for a sustainable societal change. This ideological narrative was also shared by the anti-apartheid activists in SOMAFCO and Dakawa.

SOMAFCO and Dakawa were provided materials, technical and professional assistance from countries across the Cold War borders. Solidarity workers at Mazimbu and Dakawa came from Australia, Cuba, Denmark, Finland, the GDR, Great Britain, the Netherlands, Nigeria, Norway, Sweden, Tanzania, Zambia, Guyana, Poland, Tonga, Ireland and the United States of America.[17] From a historical perspective, the centres showcased an example of a collaborative endeavour that overcame geopolitical frontlines in service of a shared ideological fight. This section focuses on donor projects undertaken by the Nordic countries, particularly Finland, but also by GDR citizens, who were active in grass-root organisations.

A visit to the Fort Hare archive in Alice, South Africa, where the documentation of South Africa's liberation struggle is kept, reveals not only the internationally shared motivation to end the apartheid rule but also the extent to which individual citizens went in their efforts to assist the centres.[18] Some of the most striking examples of the impact the ANC's anti-apartheid communication strategies had in the Global North include citizens of the GDR who went on to establish a donor relationship that persisted for many years. Donors were treated with care, and long-lasting correspondence with them was undertaken

● A product from the garment factory

by the ANC's local representatives in the centres. Such donor relationships proved to be vital for the upkeep of the centres in terms of everyday supplies and other material purposes. Although international support to the centres took place in several ways from providing construction material to technical assistance, education was one of the most popular targets of aid.

VOLUNTEERING AND MATERIAL DONATIONS

By the time SOMAFCO and Dakawa were handed over to the Tanzanian state in 1992, the centres boasted a wide range of school facilities from kindergarten to elementary school to secondary levels of education as well as vocational and adult education.[19] Educational practices at the Dakawa and SOMAFCO centres were supported by both individual citizens and non-governmental organisations (NGOs). In places such as the GDR, some citizens took initiative by organising material donations from like-minded individuals from within their local networks and sent shipments of pencils, books and other school equipment to the ANC representatives in Tanzania. In the Nordic countries, where various solidarity organisations had deep roots, fundraising and material collections were initiated through established donor organisations. Along with the shipments of goods they organised local demonstrations to support the anti-apartheid struggle and spread the ANC's publicity material in their networks.

Other forms of participation in the struggle included people from the Global North who travelled to the centres to live and work there. Over the years, a number of teachers from the Global North worked in the schools both as professional elementary school teachers and voluntary vocational tutors. Professional exchange also took place in teacher training campaigns that were organised by pedagogical centres in the Global North. Based on the University of Fort Hare's archives, such campaigns were organised in Sweden and the GDR. In practice, many educational facilities attracted both volunteers and donors of materials. For example, the Mazimbu library was supported financially by Nordic Centre Parties' Youth Organisations and on a more practical level by a Finnish librarian who worked on site. The library received around 10,000 books from global donors and served all levels of education from kindergarten to higher education.[20]

STUDENT-TO-STUDENT AND LABOUR-TO-LABOUR

When looking at the documents in Fort Hare, it soon becomes evident that many aid projects were founded on solidarity outreach among peers. Student unions, schools and pedagogical institutions directed their efforts at the schools and pupils in SOMAFCO and Dakawa. Such efforts were, from the perspective of the Global North, efforts of 'global upbringing' as much as forms of grass-root activism in a fight against oppression. For example, the Operation Day's Work (ODW) mission has a long history of collecting funds in elementary schools in the Nordic countries by getting elementary students themselves involved. The organisation was founded in Norway in 1961 after the death of UN Secretary General Dag Hammarskjöld who was known for his peace work in the Congo basin, among other projects. Supporting SOMAFCO and Dakawa was the ODW's major aim in 1985.[21] The ODW still operates in schools across the Nordic countries on an annual basis. Another example of peer-based thinking is the National Union of University Students in Finland (SYL). The Student Union supported the ANC by sponsoring a teacher in the SOMAFCO primary school, by providing some learning materials for the school and by financing a scholarship for ANC students who could then study at the Faculty of Education of the University of Jyväskylä, Finland.[22]

Some forms of adult education took place in the centres' industrial facilities that aimed at not just teaching a vocation to some of the residents but simultaneously supporting the goal of self-reliance in terms of production. The carpentry and garment workshops were both locations of vocational training but simultaneously served the purpose of local production of furniture and clothes for those living in the centres. For example, the carpentry workshop was supported by Finnish labour unions for professionals in technical fields and woodwork (operating at the time under the names Teknisten liitto and Puutyöväen liitto), meaning that a small part of the membership fee paid by the members of these unions was directed to the ANC's liberation struggle.[23] Similar labour class solidarity can be found in a bus project that was organised by the Association of Finnish Adult Education Organisation. A 39-seat school bus was manufactured in the Kutter bus factory in Finland.

The General Manager
Kutter Company
HELSINKI
Finland

Dear Sir

On behalf of the students and staff of our school, I would like to
thank you very much for the marvellous bus you have built especially
for our students. I am aware of the precious spare time you spent on
the bus.

Our children - nursery, primary and secondary levels - are the victims
of the internationally-hated apartheid system of South Africa. Today
most of the progressive people of the world have been celebrating the
defeat of fascism in Germany which has brought relative peace to the
world. We, the Blacks of South Africa, unfortunately are still feeling
the pangs of fascism in the form of apartheid, which is identical to
Nazism. Look at what is happening to my people in South Africa today!
We are yearning to go back to our motherland. But first of all apartheid
has to be destroyed with the moral, political and material support the
African National Congress is getting from people like the workers of
Kutter. Our children for whom the bus has been donated will never forget
you when they get back to South Africa. Dear friends, we look forward
to the day when your children will visit our beautiful country when it
is liberated from the apartheid monster.

Lastly dear friends, your solidarity will forever remain dear to our
troubled hearts. PEACE is the only guarantor to man's understanding
and social upliftment. It is the pivot of life.

Thank you very much for your practical solidarity with our school.

                              Peace and Friendship!

                              T K Maseko
                              Principal

cc: The Director, SOMAFCO, Tanzania

● Principal Tim Maseko's letter to the Kutter factory,
10 May 1985

As an act of solidarity for the ANC, some of Kutter's workers manufacturing the bus chose to work eight hours without salary.[24] The ANC's representative Principal Tim Maseko's letter to the Kutter factory demonstrates how such forms of 'practical solidarity', for instance a school bus, became interwoven with the wider ideological aims of liberated education in future South Africa.

CONCLUSION

It is well known that decolonisation processes in Africa were seen by both Eastern and Western Bloc as an opportunity to establish diplomatic and economic ties, aiming at gaining political influence on the continent. Africa became an arena in which the two blocs confronted each other, either by exerting soft power or plainly pursuing proxy wars. On the other hand, even though many historians relegate the Eastern Bloc's position towards Africa as solely driven by self-interest, some outstanding solidarity practices and programmes, such as the GDR's Freie Deutsche Jugend's (FDJ) long term commitment to volunteering at SOMAFCO and Dakawa, blunt such charges. As demonstrated by our research findings presented earlier, a nuanced eye is needed in order to arrive at a fair picture that does justice to individuals' particular motivations and to ANC agency in making the best out of its networks and resources in those very particular circumstances.

From a macro-perspective, it is important to note that from the 1980s onwards, Africa including Tanzania,[25] was pressured to stop its socialist experiments and embrace the liberalisation of its economies, especially through structural adjustments by institutions like the World Bank and the International Monetary Fund. The consequence was the privatisation of (almost) everything including education. The simultaneous weakening and dissolution of the Eastern Bloc from the late 1980s on meant that the ANC could no longer depend on the Soviet Union for weaponry and political support. It also meant that the apartheid government could no longer cynically justify itself as protecting the region from a 'total onslaught' or 'red danger'.[26] Both sides had to meet at the negotiating table, resulting in the ANC ban being lifted in 1990 and apartheid laws finally rescinding in 1991, opening the way for South Africa's first multiracial democratic elections three years later. Oliver Tambo handed SOMAFCO and Dakawa over to the Tanzanian government in 1992 'as monuments of solidarity and friendship,' a bit less than a year before his death. The time of exile was over.

Essi Lamberg, Lucas Rehnman

Education as resistance

Revisiting the anti-apartheid history through the South African educational camps in Tanzania inspired me to be part of the movement 'Africans need to tell their own stories'. Africa's cultural and economic contributions have for so long been documented from a Global North perspective. Is that to say, the very same colonial master nations are the ones who mysteriously brought about Africa's liberation while the effort and struggles of our fathers, 'the freedom fighters,' to build a prosperous continent will remain unpublicised or just disregarded?

This essay is an attempt to bring to light, with examples, some aspects of the specific South African anti-apartheid movement's history in Tanzania, its brother country. A man's brotherly feelings are feelings of love and loyalty, which you expect a brother to show, and indeed there is a long-lived relationship between these two nations fostered by our fathers (the freedom fighters).

Tanzania's support for liberation movements went beyond rhetoric cheering for African unity and solidarity. The nation offered itself as a base for liberation fighters, accommodating the influence not only of the African National Congress (ANC) but also the Pan African Congress (PAC) from South Africa. Mwalimu Julius Nyerere, the first president of Tanzania, and his government took action to challenge the white minority rule in South Africa while the Organisation of African Unity (OAU) announced in the 1970s that its member states would break off diplomatic relations with Britain if they did not intervene to remove the minority-controlled government. When the British government failed to do so, Tanzania was one of the few members that made good on the promise to end diplomatic relations and in doing so sacrificed £7.5 million in aid from Britain.[1]

The support came from a deeper place than just political interest. Tanzanians were used to providing charitable assistance to South Africans by way of agricultural produce, economic resources and even blood donations.[2] This generosity was prevalent notwithstanding the economic problems the country faced in the first few years after independence. Speaking at the Tanganyika African National Union (TANU) National Conference in 1967, Nyerere avowed that 'total African liberation and total African unity are basic objectives of our party and our government … we shall never be really free and secure while some parts of our continent are still enslaved.'[3]

When talking about the South African educational camps, the name Anna Abdallah cannot go unmentioned. While serving as the district commissioner of Morogoro, she planted a 'friendship tree' at the boarding school for South African emigrees in Mazimbu and visited it on a regular basis. She made it her goal to establish Mazimbu as a globally renowned destination, putting it on the global map everywhere she travelled. Anna Abdallah became an unofficial ambassador of the ANC after championing its cause and spreading awareness of its presence. During Abdallah's tenure in the Ministry of Home Affairs, she permitted the usage of extra land in Dakawa, at the time an undeveloped area a bit further to the south in Tanzania, to provide more room for ANC members who did not attend the Mazimbu institution.

● Mama Anna Abdallah (centre), regional commissioner from Morogoro, assists with digging the foundations for the children's centre in Mazimbu, Tanzania, early 1980s

Anna believed that one day South Africans would be free, they would go back home and all the facilities would benefit the people in the region of Morogoro. Eventually, on 9 July 1992, when ANC President Oliver Tambo handed over the two settlements to the Tanzanian President Ali Hassan Mwinyi, he expressed the hope that the two settlements would remain symbols of the friendship and solidarity between the peoples of Tanzania and South Africa.[4]

● Joint demonstration of Tanzanians and South Africans to celebrate Tanzania's independence day in Morogoro, Tanzania

While the apartheid rule in South Africa ended in May 1992, Tanzania transitioned from single-party rule under the Revolutionary Party to a multi-party system, and in October 1995 presidential and parliamentary elections were held for the first time in a multi-party system. Tanzania is said to be one of the politically most steadfast countries in Africa. Since the introduction of the multi-party system, the political and social circumstances have stayed relatively stable under the governance of the Party of the Revolution CCM (Chama Cha Mapinduzi). Since South Africa's transition to democracy in 1994, Tanzania and South Africa have built a solid bilateral relationship. South Africa is a strategic partner of Tanzania, with strong collaboration in the areas of health, education, environment and digital economy.

In conclusion, the determination to help this brother country was staunch and is to me one of the stories of African history and culture that debunk the myths and reveal the misconceptions that Western societies have about Africa's independence and its people's unity. The misrepresenting narrative tends to describe the negative, the awkward, the weird and the absurd. The fact remains, as portrayed earlier, that these images are not all what Africa was and is about.

Esther Mbibo

REFRAMING TRANSNATIONAL IDENTITIES: EDUCATION IN A TRANSITORY STATE

The intimate link between people and place is a recognised, anthropological need. To be naturally tied to a place is to have a stable core for one's identity and a firm cultural relativity. Territorial displacement or being exiled therefore adds complexity to the ways in which people assert their personal identity[1] and construct one for the place of their origin or temporary residence. In the case of the South African exiles in Tanzania, their identities were regularly in flux–having to move to several cities before settling in Mazimbu and most of them having changed their names for security purposes. This was further complicated by the nature of their relationship with the African National Congress (ANC), a liberation movement and political party, and by their being the guardians of the group of mostly minors. The party was often referred to in correspondence and project reports as the 'African National Congress of South Africa,' unlike other project participants referenced by their countries' names only. This characterisation gave further credence to the ANC not only as custodians of the exiled group but also as the government of a transitory state within Tanzania. This manifested in several ways. The 'citizens' of the ANC state adopted a lifestyle at the settlement that reflected the ethos of the ANC manifesto, the Freedom Charter. Furthermore, many aspects of daily life mirrored the regimented nature of lifestyles in pre-existing ANC military camps in other African ally states.[2] Consequently, new identities emerged from these conditions. They were intended to challenge the ones imposed by the apartheid regime and equip future, ideal citizens for a democratic South Africa to where the students would eventually return. Similarly, the educational system was distinctly aligned to the transitory state's governing principles. Education, as seen by the ANC, was a tool of resistance that would directly challenge the limiting beliefs of Bantu Education and was a retaliation for the apartheid Afrikaans Medium Decree of 1974 that instigated the 1976 Soweto Uprising leading to the exile of what became the residents of the Solomon Mahlangu Freedom College (SOMAFCO). A revolutionary education system, therefore, was structured to reinvent the identities of students who had up to that point been subject to a false, politically constructed characterisation.

The reports for the ANC Education Council reflected this intent in the school's educational manifesto and integrated it into activities assigned to students from pre-school to high school. This is an excerpt from the primary school division report:[3]

'Our schooling system is the alternative to Bantu education. And Bantu education is not merely a watered-down version of academic tuition: It is a schooling system which seeks to impart certain attitudes towards self and society. Our system therefore should not concentrate purely on one aspect – the academic – but should seek to foster a complete alternative value system as implied in the ANC Education Policy.'

The report further states that 'students at whatever age [are] integrated into the productive processes in the complex,' referring to the technical and industrial skills included in the formal and social education of all students. These vocational skills were also taught to promote a culture of custodianship and respect for 'socially necessary labour' in the hopes of creating a self-sustaining and independent community. The ANC's SOMAFCO syllabus was an expanded form of education that drew from traditional subjects, which prepared graduates for an international education but also social behaviours rooted in South African traditions to establish post-apartheid or democratic identities. So, although suspended between nations, a students' identity could be rooted in the principles of the transient state in preparation for a permanent future one.

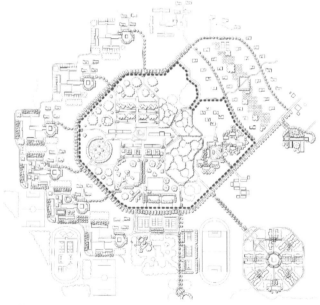

● Masterplan of SOMAFCO

Students were taught to respect themselves and others equally through exercises of cooperation and using the language and physical gestures of *ubuntu*, a Southern African concept of humanity and solidarity. Embodied speech and cultural expression are common in many South African tribes and often distinguish individuals who have stronger ties to the traditions of their homelands from the more urbanised, migrant communities (which the students from Soweto came from).

South African customs were listed as the top educational objective in the kindergarten school programme in the report for the ANC educational board. Among the subjects taught were tribal languages, traditional songs and dances and forms of oral tradition which, much like the embodied speech practice, were not normally included in curricula back in South Africa. Creating syllabi that formalised the cultural practices was a form of social constructionism that sought to naturalise behaviours traditionally learned through informal, social and familial instruction. Additionally, patriotic subjects and practices like studying history and becoming aware of the significance of the national anthem and the flag were all meant to represent the ANC as a nation state counterbalancing apartheid South Africa and its national symbols.

This socialisation was further entrenched in the manner in which the community was spatialised. The school was a carefully planned and structured environment, and the master plan of the SOMAFCO settlement had the school buildings at its centre. It was the first community in Mazimbu, a small town in the district of Morogoro, and bore the same name as the school.

The educational campus was the focal point of the site, and housing, cultural, recreational and industrial buildings were designed along roads that lead to and radiate from it. The formal circulation routes reinforced this hierarchy and guided pedestrians to the community's symbolic centre. The design was a departure from apartheid town planning that concerned itself with the surveillance of its inhabitants and was often conceptually panoptic. At SOMAFCO, the future residential development in particular could expand outwards towards the periphery of the site and follow a radial pattern of connected but independent units. The school building was planned down to the last detail.

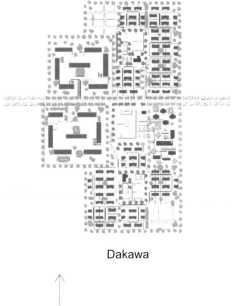

Dakawa

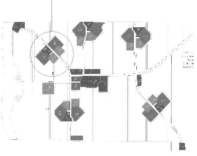

● Dakawa in relation to SOMAFCO

The campus design was perceived a success, was modified slightly and replicated in the Dakawa Development Centre, a new campus built to accommodate the throng of students that kept arriving from South Africa.

Dakawa was designed at a significantly larger scale retaining the radial design and developed according to the changing demands of the ANC state. Resources were required to support the growing communities, and so infrastructure and agricultural lands were more expansive on this particular site. This would keep both Dakawa and SOMAFCO the autonomous communities they aimed to be.[4] It also resonated with the ANC's identity in Tanzania, and like most of its state principles, this permeated the students' way of life. The student population in Dakawa leaned towards a more vocational education that in part served or prepared to serve the transient state. In this second building phase of the campus and settlement, a shooting range and guerrilla training area were included, reflecting the state of affairs back in South Africa and the ANC's consistent response to it by influencing the identities of its communities.

The ANC's transient state made nation-building a universal endeavour through deliberate planning of its social and educational programmes and spaces in the effort to challenge artificial barriers of class and race. The experimental settlement became a utopian state in which young exiles could be re-socialised as citizens of a democratic state that was yet to come – a fate hoped for but neither guaranteed nor in any way predictable time-wise. The place, though provisional, made a lasting impact on the small population of Mazimbu on the sites of abandoned, colonial sisal fields. They had to live with the tension of living on non-native land, on Tanzanian soil.

Nokubekezela Mchunu

A living experiment

Baustelle WPC-"Kindergarten" Gemeinschaftsküche
27.1.89

● Reverse of a photograph with an inscription by Jürgen Leskien, FDJ brigade

BAUSTELLE WPC-'KINDERGARTEN'
VIEWS OF THE DAKAWA DEVELOPMENT CENTRE

From 1982 to 1992, African National Congress (ANC) members constantly tried to create a temporary home for themselves in Tanzania. The Education Orientation Centre Dakawa near Morogoro was planned as a small town for nearly 5,000 refugees, consisting of houses, schools, nurseries, factories and farming land.

In contrast to the Solomon Mahlangu Freedom College (SOMAFCO), an education centre for the best students preparing for further academic education abroad, Dakawa with its orientation and vocational training centres (VTC) aimed to train future South African craftsmen: concrete workers, masons, carpenters and other tradesmen.[1]

This essay focuses on the building of the children's day care centre in the Dakawa camp using the wall panel column (WPC) construction system from the German Democratic Republic. It is narrated through archival photographs and relies on oral history stories of former inhabitants: comrades, freedom fighters, refugees, mothers, builders and volunteers. The authors of the photographs are people of a nationality that was about to be built—South African, and a nationality that would soon disappear—East German.

'A particular advantage of the testimony of images is that they communicate quickly and clearly the details of a complex process, printing for example, which a text takes much longer to describe while staying more vaguely.'[2]

Photographs from Dakawa depicting construction sites, developments and healthy community life in Africa at the end of the 1980s were very different from what was usually circulated in the mass media: famine, poverty and violence. They shocked ignorant people but also pleased donors of the project. Selected photographs reflect different views. First, official ANC and GDR photographs were taken mostly by South African students and reprinted in propaganda materials and internationally distributed brochures. Second, there are photographs from family archives of two South African-East German families living in the camp.

'When photographs come out of the storage, it is as if energy is released.'[3]

● The front of a photograph showing the construction of a
day care centre; Jürgen Leskien, album with photos of GDR
buildings in Dakawa

ARCHITEKTUR

der DDR   9/89

40 Jahre
Architekturentwicklung
in der DDR

Aufbau des ANC-Entwicklungszentrums Dakawa in Tansania

Die DDR-Solidaritätsaktion zur Unterstützung des Aufbaus des ANC-Entwicklungszentrums Dakawa/Tansania im Rahmen eines HABITAT-Projektes als Beitrag der DDR zum internationalen Jahr „Unterkünfte für die Obdachlosen" IYSH

Dipl.-Arch. Peter Wurbs

Der Afrikanische Nationalkongreß (ANC), die traditionsreichste und weltweit anerkannte Befreiungsbewegung Südafrikas, wurde 1912 gegründet. Seit seiner Gründung ist der ANC verboten und führt seinen gerechten Kampf unter illegalen Bedingungen im Heimatland und aus dem Exil. Die Leitung des ANC unter Führung seines Präsidenten Oliver Tambo hat ihr Hauptquartier in Lusaka (Republik Sambia).

Die ungerechten und unmenschlichen Bedingungen in Südafrika bewegten viele Menschen der schwarzen Bevölkerung dazu, ihr Land zu verlassen. Das zwingt den ANC, Flüchtlingslager in den Frontstaaten Afrikas für seine Anhänger einzurichten und zu unterhalten, so auch in Tansania.

1979 stellte die Regierung Tansanias dem ANC Farmland einer ehemaligen Sisalplantage in der Nähe ihrer zweitgrößten Stadt, Morogoro, zum Aufbau einer für den ANC in Zukunft sehr bedeutsamen Schule – das Solomon Mahango Freedom College – zur Verfügung. Dafür errichtete der ANC das Flüchtlingslager Mazimbu. Mazimbu war der Ausgangspunkt für den Aufbau des zweiten ANC-Flüchtlingslagers Dakawa in Tansania, 55 km nördlich von Morogoro gelegen, dessen Bau 1983 vom ANC beschlossen wurde.

1984 erarbeitete die norwegische Planungsgesellschaft NORPLAN einen Flächennutzungsplan sowie städtebauliche Bebauungsstudien für den Stand-

1 Die ersten drei Kindereinrichtungen in der WPC-Bauweise in Dakawa
2 Die Vorfertigungsanlage in Dakawa
3 ANC-Architekten informieren sich über die Projekte das Kinderzentrums in der WPC-Bauweise

1. The architecture was interlinked with the foreign policy of the GDR, which aimed for international recognition, differentiation from West Germany and a unique position among socialist countries contributing to globalisation processes in the post-colonial world.[4] Non-accidentally, independent Tanzania, a former colony of the German Empire, sustaining friendly relations with the socialist bloc, became the GDR's main place of interest and the export zone for its architecture. As a result, East German architects and state-owned companies left a significant trace in the urban landscape of the state governed by the creator of the socialist-inspired *Ujamaa* policy and the founding father of African socialism, Julius Nyerere.[5] In the 1980s, the ANC, a military liberation movement fighting against apartheid in South Africa, had established a worldwide network of representatives. As a result, the world—divided into capitalist, socialist and non-aligned blocs—intensively fought for the attention of the ANC, which soon overtook power in the state which was of critical importance in the geopolitical sense. The organisation, though leaning towards communism, tried to satisfy all and accepted help from across political lines. Both SOMAFCO and Dakawa were created with the contribution of Western donors with much help coming from Scandinavian countries.[6] Nevertheless, the GDR was the most devoted ally from the Eastern Bloc. Among different forms of support from ordinary Germans truly engaged in the anti-apartheid solidarity campaign 'DDR-Solidaritätsaktion', head of state Erich Honecker's politburo offered military training in facilities run by the Ministry for State Security, also known as Stasi, student scholarships at East German universities and housing prefabrication technology exported to Tanzania.

Sz v. 4. Nov. 1986

Ein erneuter Ausdruck unserer Solidarität

BAUTZEN. Am 23. Oktober trafen zwölf Angehörige des Afrikanischen Nationalkongresses (ANC) in unserer Kreisstadt ein. Grund des Aufenthaltes ist die Ausbildung zur Herstellung und Montage von Betonelementen für Wohnunterkünfte, Kindergärten, Schulen und ähnliches. Das Verfahren zur Errichtung dieser Elemente und Häuser ist eine Gemeinschaftsentwicklung der Bauakademie der DDR, Institut für Wohnungs- und Gesellschaftsbau Dresden, und des VEB EBAWE Baustoffmaschinen. Der Grundgedanke besteht darin, Entwicklungsländern einfach und billig zu fertigende Wohnunterkünfte als Selbsthilfeprogramm anzubieten. Die Ausbildung der Angehörigen des ANC erfolgt im Plattenwerk Bautzen.

Theresia Müller, Pressebeauftragte des VEB EBAWE Baustoffmaschinen

Dr. Tobisch (mit Brille) vom Institut für Wohnungs- und Gesellschaftsbau Dresden erläutert den ANC-Vertretern die künftigen Aufgaben.   Foto: Andreas Mittrach

● 'A renewed expression of our solidarity. Bautzen. On 23 October, twelve members of the African National Congress arrived in our county seat. The reason for the stay is the training in manufacturing and assembling concrete elements for housing, kindergartens, schools and the like. The procedure for erecting these elements and houses is a joint development of the Bauakademie der DDR (Architectural Academy of the GDR), the Institut für Wohnungs- und Gesellschaftsbau (Institute for Housing and Social Building) Dresden and the VEB (nationally owned company) EBAWE Baustoffmaschinen. The basic idea is to offer developing countries housing that can be produced easily and cheaply as a self-help programme. The members of the ANC will be trained in the factory in Bautzen.'

Sächsische Zeitung, 4 November 1986

The September 1989 issue of the *Architektur der DDR* magazine, published on the eve of the collapse of the Berlin Wall, celebrated 40 years of architectural development in the German Democratic Republic. Inside, an architect and an emissary of the Bauakademie der DDR reported on the construction of the ANC Development Centre in Dakawa, Tanzania.[7] The GDR offered the 'WPC way of construction' to the ANC, a system consisting of two kinds of simple concrete elements, panels and columns, which, assembled, create wall units resembling modular fences. The idea of its implementation in the camp came from the Bauakademie der DDR. Officially presented at the United Nations Centre for Human Settlements (UN-Habitat) conference by Professor Gottfried Wagner in the restored Bauhaus Building in Dessau (1988), it constituted a gift on the occasion of the 75th anniversary of the ANC and the GDR's contribution to the International Year of Shelter for the Homeless (1987). Architects Oswald Dennis and Spencer Hodgson were looking for cheap and easy building systems in which components could be produced on site without complex machinery and which could be assembled by unskilled labour. Even if it was not the only prefabrication system offered, the WPC system suited those needs perfectly. First, there was a real need to provide large amounts of decent accommodations in the camp as soon as possible. Second, it would have been a politically unwise decision to reject help from a country which invested so much in the future leaders of South Africa. Third, ANC members already studied architecture in Weimar and vocational training pedagogy in Magdeburg (Maxwell Mohale and German Mphahlele) and had established family bonds in the GDR.

As a result, a mobile prefabrication plant with basic equipment, tools, materials and project documentation for housing and social facilities was delivered to Tanzania. Before that, twelve ANC members travelled to East Germany to study construction in the panel factory in Bautzen. After returning to Dakawa, they received help from a brigade of the FDJ (Freie Deutsche Jugend – Free German Youth), South African settlers, international volunteers and Tanzanian construction workers. The first building erected was the children's day care centre.

Members of the ANC who studied architecture in the GDR were Spencer Hodgson and Sipho Njobe. The latter studied at the Hochschule für Architektur und Bauwesen (University of Architecture and Civil Engineering) in Weimar, which offered a course on 'Tropen- und Auslandsbau' (building in the tropics and in foreign countries). In consequence, the institute announced a competition for the urban development project for the ANC refugee camp in Dakawa.[8] The young architect who had left SOMAFCO to go to Weimar won second prize. As a result, from the beginning of September 1988, he spent six months working for the Bauakademie der DDR in Berlin preparing the implementation of WPC and developing specific housing types. Njobe appreciated the WPC technology, valuing its simplicity in production and implementation. However, a critical aspect concerned the application of the technology and the climatic requirements. The 5 centimetres of concrete walls did not offer sufficient protection from the intense Tanzanian sun and heat. Adding a second wall could be a solution to keep the enormous temperatures out.

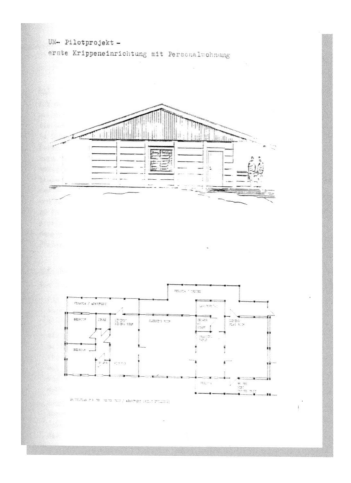

Furthermore, proper foundation and quality control checks in the factory and on the construction site could improve the final building.[9] Architect Oswald Dennis went even further, suggesting that this system could only be used for farm buildings and fencing in different conditions.[10] The truth is that Dakawa became an experimental field for architecture. It was seen as a *Neuland,* a new territory for the WPC implementation. It was driven as much by necessity as a desire to test out existing building technologies without fully considering the complex conditions. Nevertheless, imported experiments (not only from East Germany, but also from Norway) lasted only for a short time. Conventional building systems based on bricks took the lead in the final years of construction.

● Jürgen Leskien, album with photos of GDR buildings in Dakawa, 1989

● Eli Weinberg Photolab, September 1988

2. At first glance, the photograph shows three people on the construction site. They put their hands on the pile of concrete blocks used as a table to present some plans, probably architectural drawings. Behind them, there is a skeleton of the building and vertical beams resembling a concrete tree farm planted on the bare earth. On the left, some beams are already connected with larger cement panels, which are the critical elements of the WPC system. Finally, further behind, we see a finalised construction with a metal roof panelling. The building that is about to be finished here is the day care centre.

The main person in the photograph is a builder. He wears a helmet and professional looking dungarees. He points somewhere and explains something to a woman and a man in far more leisurely clothing. In white T-shirts and shorts, they look contemporary even today. A simple linen bag on the man's left arm only heightens this impression. While the woman's T-shirt seems plain, his is printed with the logo of CASA – Culture in Another South Africa, distributed during the Dutch Anti-Apartheid Movement (AAM) conference and festival in Amsterdam in December 1987.[11] The original caption of the photograph from the International Institute of Social History, Anti-Apartheid and Southern Africa Collection further explains the situation:

'Visiting Mirte de Rozario (left) and Kier Schuringa (right) from the Netherlands get an explanation about the use of prefabricated elements for the construction of houses and other buildings in the ANC Development Centre Dakawa, Tanzania.' Kier

Schuringa, back then a coordinator of the Dutch AAM education campaign, is currently an archivist of the Anti-Apartheid
and Southern Africa Collection at the International Institute
of Social History, Amsterdam. Mirte de Rozario, then a secondary school student in Huizen, had won the trip for taking
first prize in the 'Omroep voor Radio Freedom' (Broadcast-
ing for Radio Freedom) competition for which she and her
class produced a programme on South Africa.

The photograph came from the photo lab of Eli Weinberg
(1908–1981). Born to Jewish parents in the Russian Empire,
then a Latvian citizen and later South African by choice, did
not receive citizenship due to his political activism. Working
as a studio photographer first in Europe and later in South
Africa, he was an internationally celebrated artist-photogra-
pher and an active member of the South African Communist
Party. Advised by the ANC, he chose to live in exile in Dar es
Salaam where he continued his practice and took a leading
role in documenting the construction of the SOMAFCO and
Dakawa camps.[12]

'The Eli Weinberg Photolab was established by Eli himself in
the second half of the 1970s in Mazimbu, the ANC project
and refugee community in Tanzania around the Solomon
Mahlangu Freedom College (SOMAFCO), to produce photographs of Mazimbu for the ANC and the international solidarity
movement and to train SOMAFCO students in photography.
The photo archive of the Eli Weinberg Photolab was lost
after the ANC's return to South Africa in 1990. The Dutch
AAM, being one of the main solidarity groups supporting

SOMAFCO and Mazimbu, had acquired an extensive collection of printed photographs from the Eli Weinberg Photolab during the 1980s. More than 1000 photographs of Mazimbu (mostly) and Dakawa were later transferred to the IISH. The institute had them scanned and provided digital copies of these to the ANC as part of an archival project led by Kier Schuringa from 2012 to 2014.' [13]

One day during their stay with the SOMAFCO students, Mirte and Kier visited Dakawa. They took a day trip seeing a farm, the vocational training centre, textile printing workshop and the construction site. During their official activities, visitors were accompanied by one of the students from Mazimbu, a photographer whose aim it was to provide photographs to the ANC or solidarity groups needed for the documentation of the developments in Mazimbu and Dakawa.

'The guys of the Eli Weinberg Photolab worked quite informally – we didn't pose for photographs usually.' [14]

The exact authors of the photographs from the Eli Weinberg Studio are unknown. However, the names of students who decided to take photography classes must be stored in the vast archive of the ANC at Fort Hare University, together with even the slightest traces of South African life in Tanzania. Whether it was Weinberg's hand itself or the hand of one of the pupils, they knew precisely what kind of image they wanted to create and what type of situation to portray. We usually observe black heroes with sculptured bodies working together to build a safe home for the future generation of liberated South Africa.

The eye behind the lens marks out joint efforts of fighter-builders. Hand in hand, they pour concrete, install yet another concrete beam or hold a topping-out ceremony. White comrades and visitors seem to be impressed and passive observers rather than active co-workers. The construction site photographs from the workshop of Eli Weinberg prove that the ANC used the financial sources correctly and underline that the camp was built by black hands. However, could international viewers and donors recognise whether the builders were South African or Tanzanian?

'In the photograph, one of the construction workers in Dakawa—who might be an ANC member, but more likely a Tanzanian worker, as they did a lot of the construction work at the ANC projects—is explaining to Mirte and me how they worked. I remember they made the cement walls of the houses and other buildings locally and used different techniques (machines) to put them up.'[15]

On different available recordings from the construction site, one can hear that builders used various languages and spoke English with different accents. Sometimes Swahili is heard first. Then suddenly, one person says 'continue' with a distinct South African accent. In another recorded conversation English with a strong German accent can be heard from two FDJ brigade members.[16]

The labour conditions were always challenging. Nevertheless, the centre continuously grew during the 1980s. Lack of salaries, food rationing and unregular deliveries influenced all aspects of the camp's life, not to mention the construction site.

● Eli Weinberg Photolab; construction in Dakawa, 1988; photograph of the photograph by Bauhaus Lab 2022

If meals were not provided, people did not come to work. Workers also demanded siesta time and holidays, which seemed unusual in a critical situation like this.[17] German Mphahlele, GDR university alumnus and deputy principal of the VTC, recalled:

'We came with this German discipline into a very different environment. We had to find a middle road. Work had to be done, but maybe, we needed to turn down the strictness. These were not Germans.'[18]

There was a constant conflict between political aspirations and construction necessities from the very first years of the project on. The internal conflict dynamics are documented in handwritten records from the first meetings of the ANC Technical Committee in Morogoro in the spring of 1978. The discussion constantly focused on the quality of the work and workforce at Mazimbu. One of the records sums up the labour force categories: ANC comrades (with or without technical skill), local Tanzanians and skilled artisans from the international labour force (primarily volunteers), which proves the multinational character of the project. Opinions on which group was the leading force vary. In late March 1988, at the committee meeting in Morogoro, Oswald Dennis evaluated the South African comrades' skills, and the result was relatively poor for a building programme of the size of this project. Nevertheless, they agreed that as many ANC members as possible should participate in building the school because of the project's political implications.[19] That was the official policy of the ANC throughout the years: President Oliver Tambo reminded his listeners in his speeches that Dakawa was where the future builders of South Africa were being trained.

3. Annegret and Gabriele met their future husbands, German Mphahlele and Maxwell Mohale, in their homeland East Germany. Annegret (later Mphahlele) grew up in a small town near Halle and was trained as a social worker for young people. She started to work in a dormitory in Magdeburg where twelve ANC students arrived in 1981. Among them were German Mphahlele and Maxwell Mohale. Gabriele (later Mohale) grew up in Plauen and studied book printing. She met Maxwell Mohale at Alexanderplatz in Berlin at an annual solidarity bazaar. German Mphahlele and Maxwell Mohale grew up in Soweto. Mohale was a bricklayer by training. Mphahlele's education was interrupted by the Soweto Uprising. On 16 June 1976, the student protests started as a reaction to changes in the educational system of apartheid South Africa.[20] Both Mohale and Mphahlele had to flee South Africa.

Travelling between Swaziland, Mozambique and Tanzania, they spent some time in Angola for military training. Mphahlele went to Cuba and from Cuba to the GDR. Mohale went to East Germany straight from Angola. They both enrolled in the vocational training pedagogy programme in Magdeburg.[21] Both left Germany in 1987 to build a vocational training centre in Dakawa. Their wives followed them soon. In November 1988, Annegret Mphahlele arrived in Tanzania, and in February 1990, Gabriele Mohale followed with her daughter Mokgadi Mohale.

From the evening of her arrival, Annegret Mphahlele remembers the expatriates' caravan in quite luxurious conditions, as she would learn later. She was driven around on freshly

● Mokgadi Mohale standing in front of the day care centre, 1990/91

● Annegret Mphahlele with her son Poloko in the WPC constructed passage, 1991

built roads, looking through the car window, seeing the Orientation Centre, some houses in Village 4 (V4) and some factories in Village 2 (V2), hearing the voice of her husband with instructions on whom to trust and whom to talk to.[22] The presence of the FDJ brigade could have a calming effect on her, as her English was almost non-existent. However, to her surprise, people from home kept their distance.[23] You had to get permission to leave East Germany. Comrades who left the country as members of the political youth organisation kept their distance from women who had married a foreigner. Not long after arrival, she would hear mostly kids calling her 'Teacher Anna', and she became a part of the female group establishing a day care centre in Dakawa.[24]

'Initially, we started to collect kids because they were all over the place.'[25]

First, Annegret Mphahlele noticed kids playing all day in the area of her house in V4. She saw kids seeking protection from the intense afternoon sun and playing underneath a shelter. Also, she discovered where they disappeared around noon. They went to a hall full of mattresses near a house for sick comrades (Mhlaba). She wanted to know more, and she found a group of Tanzanian women, among them Mama Djupi. Then she understood. The idea was to gather the little ones and offer them a place and food. Soon she quarrelled with the storekeepers about powdered milk. The daily schedule focused on meals and naps. Breakfast in the morning, lunch at noon and then a nap. That was already a lot to organise in a refugee camp with a system of rationed goods and a shortage of professionals, especially teachers. Thanks to their persistence, a large pot of porridge was cooked, on wood, every day.[26] She and other women organised life at the construction site and adapted the day care centre built in WPC technology:

'Once, the Dan Church Aid visited [the WPC] construction site, and we showed them what we did with the little we had and how we improvised to start with some education for the young ones.'[27]

The ANC effort was appreciated soon. The first milestone was receiving a container of educational toys. These toys are visible on the colour VHS recordings made in 1989 by one of the members of the FDJ brigade, Jürgen Leskien.[28] A mixed-aged group of toddlers and some adults are outside on a sandy square in front of a wooden house with painted animal figures. The camera and its operator do not interact with their subjects. Instead, they turn to exciting moments to zoom in on and look closely at some protagonists. This way of shooting leaves the audience with a slightly disoriented feeling. It seems like only the smallest kids who were not yet able to hold on to something for a long time, did not have a toy in their hands – there were rattles, plush toys, big plastic and rag dolls, plastic animals, teddy bears, soccer and rubber balls, even a car to ride. Bright synthetic colours contrast with the natural yellow sand and the house's dark wood in the background.

The second milestone was the opening of the new building in 1990. The new day care centre was located directly on one of the main roads and was quite a central point in V2.[29]

It was planned to be part of an inter-village centre (IVC 1) connecting the villages V2 and V1.[30] As the development of V1 did not progress, the inhabitants saw the complex as part of V2. Annegret Mphahlele described the development of the day care centre project:

'We moved to a more formal set-up. Amongst other things, we started speaking to the children mainly in English.'[31]

Even more substantially, we can notice the change of attitude when we hear Gabriele Mohale talking about the day care centre. She arrived with her daughter Mokgadi Mohale in February 1990. We see how aspirations and goals grew in direct proportion to architectural progress:

'The main aim was to have all preschool children attend what is now known as early childhood education, which would prepare them well for primary school.'[32]

This centre included a kitchen with gas and electric appliances,[33] a three-part nursery with four classrooms, two staff houses and a bathroom.[34] Corner buildings had two-bedroom flats at their ends, and the middle parts served as classrooms. The building in the middle had a bathroom in-between two classrooms. The complex was completed by a round metal gazebo covered with palm leaves opposite the central building. Between the gazebo and the middle building was a playground with a plastic slide and a cement sandbox. On two sides of the playground there were concrete paths decorated with some bushes that connected the buildings with the gazebo. Another concrete path led to a cashew tree with a huge twisted trunk and round leaves, surrounded by a circular wooden bench attached to the concrete structure. The first building on the left, seen from the gazebo side, was faced by the kitchen building. In the distance, at the tree's height, there was a small zoo created on the initiative of the day care centre where two monkeys, a tortoise and a rabbit were living. Those were not the only animals present at the day care centre. Annegret Mphahlele recalled:

'At one stage we had a spitting cobra in the bushes, so one of us had to check in the morning, mostly me.'[35]

Every morning Annegret Mphahlele, the deputy principal of the day care centre, was coming for, at that time, five-year-old Mokgadi Mohale with the bus. She brought her and other kids from the V4 zone to the newly opened day care centre in V2. Mphahlele negotiated with the VTC access to a 26-seater bus to pick up supplies and children. Thanks to that, Mokgadi Mohale went to the day care centre during the day while both parents, Maxwell Mohale, at that time a VTC instructor, and Gabriele Mohale, an office administrator at the construction site office, were at work.

It was a significant change for kids and everyone who worked in the day care centre and the community. The playground, built in front of the second part of the day care centre, became an essential part of the neighbourhood as an open playground, but also as a destination for family walks at the weekend. In the photograph one of her parents took, we see Mokgadi Mohale standing in the sandpit in front of the day care centre.

Gabriele Mohale arrived in Tanzania three months after the wall between East and West Berlin had been opened on 9 November 1989. Before leaving for Tanzania, Mohale saw on German television 'the most striking symbol of the end of apartheid,' Nelson Mandela's release from prison. So the process of political changes started, but no one knew what they would look like, both in East Germany and South Africa. Then, in October 1990, the AABN video unit arrived with Dutch director Hedda van Gennep, Fons Geerlings and ANC members Zola Maseko, David Brown and Colin Belton. They shot a short documentary titled *We've come a long way.* In addition, they recorded an interview with German Mphahlele.

– You are talking about consolidating here and spreading out, how is it related to the question of repatriation and going home?
– No one can be certain that we are going home in the near future.[36]

Simultaneously, an eight-minute scene from the day care centre was filmed.[37] For around twenty kids, there are ten adults, all sitting outside on the benches around the big tree. The singing starts in Nguni languages, among them Zulo and Xhosa:

'Unyawo lami liyahamba, alisebenzeli mahala.'

The kids are running around the tree dancing and singing: 'My foot does the walking, it does not work for anything.' Later, they move in pairs towards the concrete circle surrounded by the gazebo, an excellent stage to continue the physical activities. Now, they dance around the camera person, who gently rotates to catch all the little participants. Later, they sing, clap and jump to a rhythmic chant used specifically in protest marches, one voice leading and the others joining in the chorus. While the audience is clapping, just a few kids are dancing little choreographies. We hear English: 'How are you today? I will show you the way. Sing. Tralalala-la.' Finally, we hear the voice: 'Please. Starting,' and see the right fist raised. Next, the group sings the national anthem, probably at request of the film crew. We experience the strong political context, either imposed by the visitors or successfully capturing the camp's day-to-day atmosphere. It's probably both at the same time.

● Day care centre, view of the staff house

● Development Centre Dakawa map
Photographs: Bauhaus Lab 2022

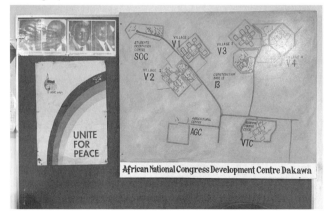

4. In 1990, Dakawa was still a construction site, focused mainly on the development of Village 2. Sipho Njobe, who arrived at Dakawa camp the same year, was working on a project of a common house with a 'tuck shop' for V2.[39] The FDJ brigade stayed in houses in V2.[40] The day care centre was already finished.

'It actually looked OK. They used just conventional roofing. It looked like other buildings. Only the structure around and inside was different.'[41] The families were moving to WPC houses in V2. Dakawa developed according to plan until 1991. Then the ANC and the donors decided to complete the current project but stop further development.[42] The Dakawa centre accommodated nearly 2,000 people by late 1991.[43] 'V2 was almost completed (83 out of 94 housing units).'[44]

The total cost of the centre was 70 million dollars. The prominent donors for the centre came from Denmark, Finland, Norway and East Germany. The South African personnel also included ex-patriates from Australia, Britain, Denmark, Finland, Germany, Nigeria and Norway. Tanzania also provided personnel, both workers and experts.[45] On 9 July 1992, Dakawa and Mazimbu were handed over to the Tanzanian government.

The authors of the text would like to thank the late Claudia Hodgson, Spencer Hodgson, Jürgen Leskien, Gabi Mohale, Maxwell Mohale, Annegret Mphahlele, German Mphahlele, Sipho Njobe, Kier Schuringa and Peter Wurbs.

Igor Bloch, Michalina Musielak

Amongst the revealing moments of our field work in South Africa, one conversation in particular remains firmly rooted in my mind. In a basement of the University of the Witwatersrand (Wits) in Johannesburg, head archivist Gabi Mohale showed us the equipment that this leading African institution had been able to acquire. In the middle of the room, there was a sizable machine that could take high-quality images of documents and objects for the digital archiving process. Purchased only a few years back, it had already become near-obsolete. That wasn't due to newer technology prevailing. The same machinery is widely used in 'western' institutions. The reason was bureaucratic: The procurement processes that Wits and most other organisations in this region are forced to go through mean purchasing from marked-up third-party sources, leaving them exposed to a lack of technical and mechanical support from the manufacturer. Gabi's response? 'In the global south, we depend on finding solutions ourselves.'

It might be a leap to link small administrative issues like this to greater colonial injustices, but it is a clear example of how the globalised system continues to work against countries that share a history of past colonialism. The playing field is far from level, and our recent visit to South Africa ingrained this in us and informed our approach to the exhibition.

Our initial destination was the Eastern Cape. Landing in East London (in Xhosa: eMonti), we collected two hire cars for the bumpy drive up to our accommodation in the Amathole Mountains. A picturesque Alpine-looking village, Hogsback was once home to Xhosa tribes before colonialism and the laws of apartheid regulated who was allowed to live here. Eventually, a tourism industry for the well-off emerged. The deep spatial legacy of apartheid, which continues to show in the reality of post-apartheid urbanism, became obvious on our drives to the nearest town of Alice, once divided into racialised zones and now almost entirely abandoned by its former White inhabitants.

Next to the town is the University of Fort Hare, an important institution through the mid-20th century with a proud legacy of being the alma mater of Nelson Mandela, Oliver Tambo, Desmond Tutu, Julius Nyerere and others. The ANC chose it as the custodian of its liberation movement archive which proved to form a guiding part of our work. Each morning we were greeted by Mr Poni, the building's security officer, before we worked our way through boxes of documents.

Senior archivist Mosoabuli Maamoe at one point took us to the object collections and told us about long-gestated plans for the institution to exhibit its considerable collection of contemporary African art. Financing and security were cited as the reasons we were the only ones who were able to view it at the time.

With the hotel's WiFi just about supporting a video call, we were able to make contact with our colleagues who were concurrently visiting the sites in Tanzania. We both stood in places fundamental to the interpretation of anti-apartheid liberation, and at a distance of 2,000 miles, we had been having similar conversations. In both countries we witnessed a strong desire at the local level to be not just a passive custodian, but an active interpreter of these histories. At Dakawa, they had been told of future hopes to welcome the public to the campus as a heritage and education site. Yet a fundamental lack of resources was making this a long-term aim. So who gets to tell these stories?

The field visits proved to be more than a mere practical opportunity for documentation and archival research, but a process for understanding the continued legacies and injustices that exist between north and south as well as east and west. It challenged us to consider our collective positionality and that of the Bauhaus in telling a story that is foremost one of African-led liberation.

Jordan Rowe

Exhibition

Doors of Learning
Microcosms of a Future South Africa
Presented at the Bauhaus Dessau
Bauhaus Lab 2022

As images of the South African regime's brutal response to anti-apartheid regulation were broadcast across the world, political and economic pressure steadily grew from abroad. This international support for this African National Congress (ANC) came from a mix of socialist nations, including the GDR, the governments of the Nordic countries, and those of newly independent African states, such as Tanzania. Often working through the framework of UN programmes, these countries provided a critical mix of financial, political, and technical support for the ANC's activities in exile, including in the development of SOMAFCO and Dakawa.

Wherever their masses and strategies differed, in conjunction with growing movements and non-governmental organisations from the rest of the world, the ANC exile centres became a highly interactive points between a Liberated and South during the Cold War.

Mit der weltweiten Ausstrahlung der Bilder der brutalen Reaktion des südafrikanischen Regimes auf die Anti-Apartheid-Opposition nahm auch der politische und wirtschaftliche Druck international zu. Vor allem sozialistische Länder (einschließlich der DDR), skandinavische Länder sowie neue unabhängige afrikanischen Staaten wie Tansania nahmen Partei für den Afrikanischen Nationalkongress (ANC) und unterstützten diesen meist, häufig im Rahmen von UN-Programmen teilten diese Länder finanzielle, politische und technische Unterstützung für die Aktivitäten des ANC im Exil, unter anderem für

die Entwicklung von SOMAFCO und Dakawa. Dabei unterschieden sich jedoch Mittel und Hilfestrategien. Hand in Hand mit wachsenden Bewegungen und Nichtregierungsorganisationen wurden Südafrikas Exil-Zentren zu überaus interaktiven.

"The Doors of Learning
and Culture Shall
Be Opened"

In the Freedom Charter
a statement of core
principles produced
by South African liberation
movements in 1955 –
it is a stated ambition that
"Higher economic ... shall
be opened to all." Inspired
by this statement, this area
provides the opportunity to
further explore and engage
with the exhibition themes.
We encourage those that
guided the curators in
the research phase, but also
invite and provoke materials
their own questions about
the formation of a new
South Africa – an apologia
to our story. You are
encouraged to add to
that evolving exhibit by
responding to the questions
and prompts, by adding new
questions and offering further
insights and feedback

In der Freedom Charter –
eine Erklärung der wichtigsten
Grundsätze der südafrikanischen Befreiungsbewegungen
aus dem Jahr 1955 – wird
unter anderem gefordert,
dass "allen der Zugang zu
höherer Bildung ... ermöglicht
werden soll". Inspiriert von
dieser Erklärung versteht sich
dieser Bereich als Einladung,
die Ausstellungsschwer-
punkte zu erkunden
und auch mit ihnen ausein-
anderzusetzen. Wir aber
laden unsere Beteiligten ein,
die Fragen zu erkunden,
die sich während der
Recherchephase ergeben
haben, um auch unsere
Geschichte zu hinterfragen
und einen eigenen Beitrag
zur Aufarbeitung dieses
neuen Südafrika zu leisten.
Dieser Ausstellungsbereich
soll sich im Laufe der
Zeit weiterentwickeln,
indem wir Fragen und Anregun-
gen, Ideen, neue Ideen und
Perspektiven einzubringen

DOORS OF LEARNING—A FILM RESPONSE

What purpose do the two settlements serve today? In what condition are the buildings? How are they used? What was it like for people in exile to attempt to build a new home while longing to go back to their old home? How do people's ideas of home and sense of belonging change under forced migration? How do memories connected to a specific space and place affect how we choose our future lives? With these questions in mind, *Doors of Learning* is filmed and exhibited as a three-channel video installation (16'10'') with a silkscreen curtain made with reference to the patterns that were used in the silkscreen workshops. The installation shares an impression of everyday life in the two settlements, SOMAFCO and Dakawa, by interweaving archival footage and documents with interview clips from South Africa and footage of the sites in Tanzania today that were filmed during the Lab's excursions to the respective countries.

Materials that show the school rules, including teaching the colours of the South African flag and singing the national anthem, offer a glimpse of how the education system was designed and carved out in the two settlements to allow those in exile to engage with their home identity. While trying to construct a new home in a foreign land, they were also always longing to go home.

PART 1: A POLITICAL PROJECT

Beginning on an orange earth road, the film takes us to a meeting before the settlements were built and puts forward examples of some of the challenges that were faced. It subsequently introduces personal accounts and memories of the first days after arriving at the schools.

● Orange earth road on a mountain looking over Morogoro, Tanzania

VOLKER
I question the apparent lack of participation from the ANC people of Morogoro in the planning of the school.

DENNIS
I agree that as many comrades as possible should participate in the building of the school, as Volker says: 'The project is a political project.'

VOLKER
We should discuss the interest and participation of the comrades in the work they are doing, whether skilled or not.

DENNIS
I insist we look at the quality of the work for two reasons. Firstly, the aim of the project is to reach a good building standard. Secondly, the aim is to use the working situation as an educational period for any craft involved right from the beginning.

TWEED
We must put the most emphasis on the matter of using the initiative of the comrades, whether skilled or unskilled, and to avoid depriving the comrades of this initiative by giving everything over to the 'fundies' from outside.

(From the minutes of a meeting of the ANC Technical Committee held on 26 March 1978)

● SOMAFCO secondary school students sang the ANC's national anthem each Friday morning in Mazimbu, Tanzania.

● 'This is the sign of power.' Mosoabuli Maamoe, senior archivist of the liberation movement archives at the University of Fort Hare, raising his arm in the power sign. He was a student in exile at the Solomon Mahlangu Freedom College (SOMAFCO) in the early 1980s and later studied in the GDR and the United Kingdom. He tells us about the difficulties of having to adapt to a new culture and environment because people coming into the camp all brought their own cultures, and it was not easy to acclimatise to the conditions of a new country. At the school, they were lacking the materials, teaching staff and accommodation necessary for studying.

● John Pampallis, former history teacher at SOMAFCO. Previously an exile in the UK and Canada, John gives an account of the first days of teaching at SOMAFCO. Even though student participation was low in the beginning, they slowly understood that the purpose of the school was a transition for them to gain education. Students were given extra physical labour if they were late for school.

PART 2: THE FOUNDATION

The rules that provided a foundation for the schools are listed against footage of the school environment in the past (provided by Jürgen Leskien) and present.

The school should be a carefully planned environment which ensures that everything has a purpose, that everything should be structured to encourage progress in learning and the promotion of the desired attitudes toward the self and society.

● SOMAFCO classroom

Never shout.

Never tell a child they are wrong or bad.

Encourage the child.

When the child is not doing their activity correctly, stay quiet until the child is finished, then start from the beginning, showing the child the correct way of doing it, encouraging them to help you. WORK AS PARTNERS. When the child gets bored or seems frustrated, stop and change the activity immediately.

In the primary division (and the nursery school when it is fully established) we are laying the real foundations of our future society, the society we envisage and want.

Practical life activities:
Buttoning
Zipping
Hooking
Shoe-lacing

Personal hygiene:
Wash your hands
Wash your face
Wash your feet
Brush your teeth
Cut your nails
Comb your hair

Personal identity:
My name is …
My mother's name is …
My father's name is …
I am a South African.
My President is Comrade President O. R. Tambo.
I belong to the ANC (S.A.).

● Mural depicting freedom fighters on the entrance wall at SOMAFCO

A pre-schooler learns politics
The flag
The teacher:
Put the colour slides in order: black, green, gold
Point to the colour and say 'black' (three times)
Point to the colour and let the children say 'black'
(three times)
Point to the following colours, following the same
methods as b) and c)
Mix the colour slides and say: 'Prudy, show me "black"';
'Oh, very good, that's a clever girl! What's this colour?
Show me "gold".'

When each child is mastering a colour, let the whole
group clap their hands, praising him or her.

● Professor Allen L. Malisa, former principal of Solomon Mahlangu College of Science and Education, shared with us the history of the school while giving us a tour of the campus. There is a monument of Oliver Tambo at the campus entrance, which was built to commemorate the friendship between Tanzania and South Africa when ANC freedom fighters were leaving to go back to South Africa in 1992.

PART 3: MONDAY

Each day of the week is carefully planned to the hour, with different activities and food prepared for different days. The film finishes with a typical Monday schedule while juxtaposing the schedule for 'going home' for the day and accounts of those who wanted to 'go home' to South Africa.

8:00–8:15
National anthem and
freedom songs

8:15–9:15
Breakfast
Porridge, milk

9:15–9:30
Folk tales

9:30–9:45
Finger-painting

9:45–10:00
Rhymes

10:00–10:30
Morning snack
Raw tomato

10:30–12:00
Playing assorted games

12:00–1:00
Lunch
Beef, rice, vegetables

1:00–3:00
Sleeping

3:00–3:30
Afternoon snack
Fruit salad

4:00
Going home

● Spencer Hodgson, Karin Pampallis (centre), secretary and administrator to Oswald Dennis, project manager of SOMAFCO, and Claudia Hodgson tell us about a news committee that monitored radio news broadcasts from various countries and compiled a news bulletin every day. This helped them to stay in touch with what was happening in the liberation struggle and in the world at large.

● Gabi Mohale, Maxwell Mohale, Annegret Mphahlele and German Mphahlele, tell us that they wanted to go home – they were on one of the first planes going back to South Africa because they wanted to be part of building their country. See pages 70-77 for a detailed account of the experiences of the Mohales and Mphahleles.

Joyce Lam

Doors of Learning
3-channel video installation with silkscreen curtain, 16' 11"
Concept and editing by Joyce Lam and Michalina Musielak
Narrator: Noland Oswald Dennis
Protagonists: Claudia Hodgson, Spencer Hodgson,
Mosoabuli Maamoe, Allen L. Malisa, Gabi Mohale,
Maxwell Mohale, Annegret Mphahlele, German Mphahlele,
Godfrey Msimbe, John Pampallis, Karin Pampallis
Archival footage (Tanzania): Jürgen Leskien
Curtain: Weronika Stasińska
Pattern design: Dariusz Wekwert
Print: Bauhaus Dessau Foundation
Installation design: Nokubekezela Mchunu

Appendix

● *Igor Bloch* is an art and architecture historian, currently a PhD Research Student at Ghent University and Vrije Universiteit Brussel. His research connects the fields of colonial and construction history with a focus on housing projects in Belgian Congo.

● *Joyce Lam* is an artist and book editor. She is interested in exploring ideas about the sense of home, memory and identity through multidisciplinary practice, focusing on documentary films, video installations and lecture performances. Her major works include *On Family* (solo exhibition, TOKAS-Emerging 2022, Tokyo Arts and Space Hongo, Japan, 2022; lecture performance, Yokohama International Performing Arts Meeting Fringe, Japan, 2021) and *The Cooked* (Tokyo Documentary Film Festival, Japan, 2021). She is a recipient of the U39 Artist Fellowship (Arts Commission Yokohama, Japan, 2022).

● *Essi Lamberg* is a doctoral researcher at the University of Helsinki. Her research area focuses on the history of development cooperation from multiple perspectives including visual and cultural studies, spatial planning and urbanism.

● *Esther Wakuru B. Mbibo* is an award-winning graduate architect from Ardhi University in Dar es Salaam, Tanzania. She is currently an independent researcher and a visionary for innovative initiatives for informal settlements in Dar es Salaam, 'Uswazi Disruptors', where she informs and organises innovative interventions to improve the living conditions of informal settlement dwellers. Her research engages documentary recording, photography, community discussions and architectural design with a focus on finding practical solutions for spatial development in underprivileged societies which will hopefully later impact Africa at large.

● *Michalina Musielak* is a Polish visual anthropologist, researcher and artist, currently a PhD candidate at the Centre for Research on Social Memory at the University of Warsaw and 'Meisterschülerin' at the HGB Leipzig. Her research engages with architecture and the memory of the 20th century which she narrates in documentary forms and curatorial projects.

● *Nokubekezela Mchunu* is an architectural researcher and designer from Johannesburg, South Africa. Her research interests and past work concern applied history. She received a scholarship as a design informant for inclusive, contemporary practice. She is particularly interested in how cultural hermeneutic approaches can contribute to democratic design. She is currently a PhD researcher at the University College of Dublin as part of an ERC-funded project, *Expanding Agency: Women, Race and the Global Dissemination of Modern Architecture*. She is a current Junior Fellow at the Architectural Histories Journal, and at the Canadian Centre for Architecture Research, she is a member of the Network Steering Committee.

● *Lucas Rehnman* is a Brazilian-born artist-researcher-curator based in Berlin, Germany. He obtained a Master of Arts degree in Public Spheres at édhéa (Valais School of

Art, Switzerland), enabled by the Hansjoerg Wyss scholarship. Since 2020 he has investigated the legacies of East-South cooperation during the Cold War and the potential lessons of modernism in Global South contexts.

● *Jordan Rowe* is a writer, curator and researcher on urban culture with a particular interest in institutions and placemaking. He has served as the first ever Urbanist in Residence at the Museum of London, was a Fellow at Theatrum Mundi and manager of the UCL Urban Laboratory.

● The entrance to the Dakawa Development Centre

● Bauhaus Taschenbuch 27
The book was published in the context of the Bauhaus Lab
2022 exhibition presented at the Bauhaus Dessau from
4 August 2022 to 8 January 2023.

● Edited by
Bauhaus Dessau Foundation
Director Dr Barbara Steiner
Gropiusallee 38
06846 Dessau-Roßlau
Telephone +49-340-6508-250
www.bauhaus-dessau.de

● Academy Team, Bauhaus Dessau Foundation:
Programme head: Dr Regina Bittner
Research associate: Philipp Sack
Student assistant: Weronika Stasińska

● Bauhaus Lab 2022 participants:
Igor Bloch, Joyce Lam, Essi Lamberg, Esther Wakuru B.
Mbibo, Michalina Musielak, Nokubekezela Mchunu, Lucas
Rehnman, Jordan Rowe

● Editing
Petra Frese, Rebecca Philipps Williams

● Translation and Copyediting
Bauhaus Lab 2022
Petra Frese, Rebecca Philipps Williams

● Project management
Katja Klaus

● Graphic design
Anne Meyer
based on a concept by HORT, Berlin
www.hort.org.uk

● Printed by
Pöge Druck, Leipzig
www.poegedruck.de

● Publisher
Spector Books, Leipzig
www.spectorbooks.com

● Distribution
Germany, Austria: GVA, Gemeinsame Verlagsauslieferung
Göttingen GmbH & Co. KG,
www.gva-verlage.de
Switzerland: AVA Verlagsauslieferung AG, www.ava.ch
France, Belgium: Interart Paris, www.interart.fr
UK: Central Books Ltd, www.centralbooks.com
USA, Canada, Central and South America, Africa
ARTBOOK | D.A.P. www.artbook.com
Japan: twelvebooks, www.twelve-books.com
South Korea: The Book Society, www.thebooksociety.org
Australia, New Zealand: Perimeter Distribution,
www.perimeterdistribution.com

The Bauhaus Dessau Foundation is a non-profit foundation under public law. It is institutionally funded by:

 Die Beauftragte der Bundesregierung für Kultur und Medien

SACHSEN-ANHALT

Dessau ⅂ Roßlau

First edition, 2023
© Bauhaus Dessau Foundation
ISBN 978-3-95905-746-2

● Front page
SOMAFCO primary school, Mazimbu, Tanzania. First
grade classroom 1983. Eli Weinberg Photolab. Anti-Apartheid and Southern Africa Collection, Amsterdam.

● Exhibtion photos
Bauhaus Dessau Foundation.
© Yvonne Tenschert

- p. 16
© UWC-Robben Island Museum, Mayibuye Archives.

- p. 18/19
© African National Congress Archive Fort Hare University,
Alice, South Africa.

- p. 20
© UWC-Robben Island Museum, Mayibuye Archives.

- p. 25
© International Institute of Social History, Anti-Apartheid
and Southern Africa Collection, Amsterdam.

- p. 29
© African National Congress Archive Fort Hare University,
Alice, South Africa.

- p. 36/38
© Eli Weinberg Photolab.

- p. 42
© Spencer Hodgson personal archive.

- p. 44/45
© Spencer Hodgson personal archive.

- p. 106
Interview with Mosoabuli Maamoe, conducted by
Esther Mbibo and Michalina Musielak,
Johannesburg, South Africa, 2 June 2022

© Bauhaus Lab 2022.

- p. 107
Joyce Lam, Mazimbu, Tanzania, 1 June 2022
© Bauhaus Lab 2022.

- p. 108
Joyce Lam, Mazimbu, Tanzania, 1 June 2022
© Bauhaus Lab 2022.

- p. 110
Joyce Lam, Dakawa, Tanzania, 3 June 2022
© Bauhaus Lab 2022.

- p. 111
Interview conducted by Esther Mbibo, Regina Bittner
and Michalina Musielak, Johannesburg,
South Africa, 5 June 2022
© Bauhaus Lab 2022.

- p. 113
Interview with Spencer Hodgson, Karin Pampallis, Claudia
Hodgson, conducted by Regina Bittner and Michalina
Musielak, Johannesburg, South Africa, 5 June 2022
© Bauhaus Lab archives.

INTRODUCTION

1 Bauakademie der DDR directive for the implementation of the seminar 'Experience of the GDR in solving the housing problem and its relevance for developing countries', 1988, Archives of the Bauhaus Dessau Foundation, collection number EA 264_fundus.
2 Peter Wurbs. 'Aufbau des ANC-Entwicklungszentrums Dakawa in Tansania', in *Architektur der DDR* 9/1989, pp. 51–54.
3 Inv. A2_2 International cooperation, IRS Scientific Collection, collection number A2_2_14.
4 See annotation 2
5 National Heritage and Cultural Studies (NAHECS), University of Fort Hare, ANC Archives, collection number SDO/049/0014/120.
6 See *inter alia* Steffi Marung, James Mark and Artemy M. Kalinovsky (eds.). *Alternative Globalizations. Eastern Europe and the Postcolonial World.* Bloomington: Indiana University Press, 2020.

ANTI-COLONIAL EDUCATION AND SOLIDARITY IN THE ANC EXILE CENTRES

1 It established offices across the world, from Zambia and Tanzania to Canada, the UK and the GDR, among other countries.
2 Botswana, Lesotho, Mozambique, Swaziland, Angola, Zambia, Zimbabwe and Tanzania, for example, all played an important role in supporting the ANC's liberation struggle.

3 Just to illustrate such dangers as very real: Mozambican anti-colonial leader Eduardo Mondlane was killed by a bomb in 1969, clearly the work of pro-Portugal secret intelligence. 'Portuguese, Rhodesian, and South African agents sought to subvert the guerrilla organisations and destabilise the Tanzanian political scene [...] Dar es Salaam's public sphere was rife with [Cold War] gossip: Nyerere himself dubbed the city "Rumourville".' In George Roberts. *Eduardo Mondlane in Dar es Salaam: tour d'horizon of a 'Cold War city'*. LSE/GWU/UCSB International Graduate Conference on the Cold War, London 2015. Also, in 1989, in Zambia, an ANC farm named Chongela was attacked by pro-apartheid mercenaries, resulting in many deaths.

4 Oral account by Prof. Allen Lewis Malisa.

5 The most comprehensive study on SOMAFCO, *Education in Exile – the ANC School in Tanzania, 1978 to 1992* by Séan Morrow, Brown Maaba and Loyiso Pulumani (Cape Town: HSRC, 2004), states that 'the idea of a school for exiles was not new within the ANC' and that 'the outflow of young exiles from 1976 [...] made it possible to implement an idea that was clearly already in the air'. Unanimous among scholars and oral accounts is the importance of Oliver Tambo (1917–1993) to its foundation. Tanzanian Professor Allen Lewis Malisa, former Principal of the Solomon Mahlangu College of Science and Education (now College of Natural and Applied Sciences) at the Sokoine University of Agriculture, told us that the newly-arrived 'youth found themselves away from home with very little to do, so they sat in groups, [and] the older ones started to teach younger ones. When this information reached

the ANC leaders, in particular, Oliver Tambo, he was so touched that he ordered a school to be built in this area.'

6 Tanzanian politician Anna Abdallah (b. 1940) has worked for women's rights, changed the gender-biased Tanzanian criminal justice system, supported indigenous language education and also fought for the rights of ethnic minorities. As Morogoro district commissioner, she was instrumental in establishing SOMAFCO, planted a 'friendship' tree in the surroundings and visited the centre on a regular basis. She made it a goal to establish SOMAFCO as a globally renowned destination, putting it on the global map everywhere she travelled. She became an unofficial ambassador of the ANC after championing its cause and spreading awareness of its activities. During Abdallah's tenure in the Ministry of Home Affairs, she permitted the usage of extra land in Dakawa to provide more room for South African exiles.

7 In *SOMAFCO's progress report,* special edition, Historical Papers Research Archive, Wits University, Johannesburg.

8 In *Recalling the construction of our ANC Centres in Tanzania – Mobilising global solidarity with the people of South Africa,* written account by Spencer Hodgson, 'draft version 5', unpublished.

9 In Tim Maseko. *NEDUC 5 Report – Report of the Principal on the Secondary School.*

10 An approach aiming at bridging the gap between mental and manual labour, developed by anti-apartheid activist and education theorist Patrick van Rensburg (1931–2007). 'A genuine alliance between learning and production, be

tween mind and labour', in the words of Oliver Tambo. In such an approach, concerned with attaining societal self-sufficiency, weaving, carpentry, building, horticulture and mechanics were given the same importance as 'strictly' academic subjects.

11 See PAIGC educational initiatives during Guinea-Bissau's liberation struggle, such as the schools in the liberated zones and the boarding schools known as *escolas-piloto* in Guinea-Conakry and Senegal.

12 *Ujamaa* (meaning 'fraternity' in Swahili) was a socialist ideology that formed the basis of Julius Nyerere's development policies. It means cooperative economics in the sense of local people cooperating with each other to provide for the essentials of living or to build and maintain people's own stores, shops and other businesses and to profit from them together.

13 'A process by which two cultural forms (e.g. religious, intellectual, political or economic) having certain similarities or kinships enter into a relationship of reciprocal attraction and/or influence and/or mutual reinforcement.' The parts/actors/agents concerned may not be consciously aware of the affinity. In Michael Löwy. 'The concept of elective affinity used by Max Weber', *Archives de sciences sociales des religions,* vol. 127, issue 3, 2004.

14 This was also one of Amílcar Cabral's key concerns: 'Fighting with arms in one's hands isn't enough. It's necessary to struggle with political consciousness in one's head. It's necessary that we be aware that it's the consciousness of a man that guides the gun, and not the gun that guides his consciousness. The gun counts because

the man is behind it, grasping it. And it's worth more the more the consciousness of the man is worth, the more the man's consciousness serves a well-defined, clear, and just cause.' In Amílcar Cabral. *Analysis of a Few Types of Resistance,* 1969, later published as *Resistance and Decolonization.* London: Rowman & Littlefield International, 2016.

15   In Séan Morrow, Brown Maaba, Loyiso Pulumani. *Education in Exile – SOMAFCO, the ANC School in Tanzania, 1978 to 1992. C*ape Town: HSRC Press, 2004, p. 96.

16   Many Nordic solidarity movements had their roots in youth culture and the 'global awakening' of the 1960s in the Global North. In Finland, for example, student movements were at the forefront of the Cold War ideological fight and anti-colonial protests that were often seen not just as liberation struggles but also as class struggles.

17   *Education for Liberation, The Solomon Mahlangu Freedom College 10 Years, 1979–1989,* University of Fort Hare, ANC Archives.

18   The Bauhaus Lab 2022 visited the University of Fort Hare's archive in May 2022. The findings discussed in this article are the outcome of research conducted on files organised according to the ANC's supporters' nationality, showcasing examples of international solidarity, some of which were presented in the exhibition *Doors of Learning: Microcosms of a Future South Africa* (4 August 2022 to 8 January 2023, Dessau, Germany). See Fort Hare, African National Congress Archives; ANC Somafco, Director's Office; Countries. Our research in the Fort Hare archives is supplemented by findings from Työväen arkisto (The Labour Archives) in Helsinki, Finland. Findings from

the Labour Archives reveal how NGOs like Solidaari-
suus (International Solidarity Foundation), Taksvärkki
(Dagsverke, Operation Day's Work) or Suomen yliooppi-
laskuntien liitto (National Union of University Students in
Finland) supported the fight against apartheid.

19 *The ANC's SOMAFCO Progress Report, Special Edition,*
1985. Hilda and Rusty Bernstein Papers, 1931–2006,
University of Fort Hare, ANC Archives, collection number A3299.

20 *Recalling the construction of our ANC Centres in Tanzania – Mobilising global solidarity with the people of South
Africa,* written account by Spencer Hodgson, 'draft version 5', unpublished.

21 Timo Voipio. 'Kutterin koulubussi on jo Afrikassa', *Län-
siväylä,* 2 June 1985, University of Fort Hare, ANC Archives.

22 SYL's secretary for development cooperation Tuija Hal-
mari's letter to Tim Maseko, 5 January 1988, University
of Fort Hare, ANC Archives.

23 Leo Söderqvist. 'Mazimbussa valmistaudutaan tulevai-
suuden muutoksiin', *Tekniset,* 7/1990, pp. 22–24.

24 Helena Kekkonen's letter to Tim Maseko, 2 January 1985,
University of Fort Hare, ANC Archives.

25 By the early 1980s, Tanzania was facing a complex economic crisis that 'forced' the government to abandon its
socialist principles.

26 De Wet Potgieter. *Total Onslaught: Apartheid' s Dirty Tricks
Exposed.* Cape Town: Zebra Press, 2007.

TANZANIA – THE PLAYGROUND, BROTHERLY LOVE

1 Ali Mazrui, Lindah L. Mhando. *Julius Nyerere: Africa's Titan on a Global Stage.* Durham: Carolina Academic Press, 2013, p. 309.
2 Ibid. p. 167.
3 Colin Legum, G. R. V. Mmari (eds.). *Mwalimu: The Influence of Nyerere.* Dar es Salaam: Mkuki na Nyota, 1995, p. 164.
4 *African Affairs,* vol. 115, issue 460, July 2016, pp. 584–586.

REFRAMING TRANSNATIONAL IDENTITIES: EDUCATION IN A TRANSITORY STATE

1 Cathrine Brun. 'Reterritorializing the Relationship between People and Place in Refugee Studies', *Geografiska Annaler,* series B, Human Geography, vol. 83, no. 1 (2001), pp. 15–25.
2 Archival report with timetable demonstrating lessons and behaviours that confirm this. Also, an oral account by current Dakawa Development Centre official Godfrey Msimbe who stated the latter. SOMAFCO became increasingly regimented in how incoming students were commanded and instructed. Dakawa's master plan supports this in its fragmented layout that resembles a process map through which students would sequentially make their way.
3 From an educational report from the Fort Hare Archives.
4 Séan Morrow. 'Dakawa Development Centre: An African National Congress Settlement in Tanzania, 1982–1992', *African Affairs,* 1998.

BAUSTELLE WPC-'KINDERGARTEN' VIEWS OF THE DAKAWA DEVELOPMENT CENTRE

1 Lars Jakob Nerg, Wenche Svela, Daryl Sturrock. *Report from African National Congress (SA)'s Vocational Training Centre, Dakawa – Tanzania 1988–1992. From Practical Skills to Trade Education, 16 June 1992.* University of Fort Hare, ANC Archives, inventory: Director's office. Solomon Mahlangu Freedom College, no. 12, Mazimbu Project, 1978–1981, Alice, Box 68, SDO\044\0005\3, p. 8.

2 Peter Burke. *Eyewitnessing, The Uses of Images as Historical Evidence.* London: Reaktion Books, 2019, p. 83.

3 Patricia Hayes. 'Photography history and memory', in Wolfram Hartmann, Jeremy Silvester, Patricia Hayes (eds.). *The Colonising Camera.* Cape Town: University of Cape Town Press, 1999.

4 *Alternative Globalizations?* Lecture, Steffi Marung (Leipzig University), Bauhaus Lab, Bauhaus Dessau Foundation, 19 May 2022.

5 *The role of GDR architects in global development programs,* lecture, Andreas Butter (IRS Erkner), Bauhaus Lab, Bauhaus Dessau Foundation, 17 May 2022.

6 For instance, Norwegian contractor NORPLAN, with an office in Dar es Salaam, monopolised all projects financed by the Norwegian aid committee.

7 Peter Wurbs. 'Aufbau des ANC-Entwicklungszentrums Dakawa in Tansania', *Architektur der DDR,* 9/1989,pp. 51–54.

8   Hochschule für Architektur und Bauwesen. Weiterbildungs-institut für Städtebau und Architektur. *Wissenschaftliche Ergebnisse aus Lehre und Forschung.* WBI no. 96, Scientific Collections, IRS Archiv, Erkner, R 4264/96 W.

9   Sipho Njobe, interview conducted by Regina Bittner and Michalina Musielak, Johannesburg, South Africa, 4 June 2022, Bauhaus Lab archives.

10 D. Hincks, MSAAD. *Evaluation Report on Dan Church Aid to ANC Centres Mazimbu and Dakawa in Tanzania,* 31 October 1988. University of Fort Hare, ANC Archives, inventory: Director's office. Solomon Mahlangu Freedom College, no. 12, Mazimbu Project, 1978–1981, Alice, Box 68.

11 Kier Schuringa, interview conducted by Michalina Musielak, email message to Michalina Musielak, 28 March 2022, Bauhaus Lab archives.

12 Kier Schuringa. 'Copyrights enquiry', email message to Michalina Musielak, 12 July 2022.

13 'Eli Weinberg', *South African History Online.* https://www.sahistory.org.za/people/eli-weinberg. 2 April 2023.

14 *Anti-Apartheids Beweging Nederland Photo Collection.* https://search.iisg.amsterdam/Record/COLL00149. 2 April 2023.

15 Kier Schuringa, interview conducted by Michalina Musielak, email message to Michalina Musielak, 28 March 2022, Bauhaus Lab archives.

16 Ibid.

17 Archiv Demokratischer Sozialismus, inventory: project 'Die Solidarität der DDR und der BRD mit dem südafrikanischen Befreiungskampf', Rosa-Luxemburg-Stiftung, Berlin, 2020-13-39.

18 Annegret Mphahlele, German Mphahlele, Gabriele Mohale, Maxwell Mohale, interview conducted by Esther Mbibo and Michalina Musielak, Johannesburg, South Africa, 4 June 2022, Bauhaus Lab archives.

19 Ibid.

20 ANC – Technical Committee, Morogoro, 26 March 1978, 12 April 1978, University of Fort Hare, ANC Archives, inventory: Director's office. Solomon Mahlangu Freedom College, no. 12, Mazimbu Project, 1978–1981, Alice, Box 68, SDO/068/00/2/2.

21 'The Youth Struggle', *South African History Online,* 7 August 2019, https://www.sahistory.org.za/article/youth-struggle

22 Annegret Mphahlele, German Mphahlele, Gabriele Mohalej, Maxwell Mohale, introductory part of the interview conducted by Esther Mbibo and Michalina Musielak, Johannesburg, South Africa, 4 June 2022, Bauhaus Lab archives.

23 Lars Jakob Nerg, Wenche Svela, Daryl Sturrock. *Report from African National Congress (SA)'s Vocational Training Centre, Dakawa – Tanzania 1988–1992. From Practical Skills to Trade Education, 16 June 1992.* University of Fort Hare, ANC Archives, inventory: Director's office. Solomon Mahlangu Freedom College, no.12 Mazimbu Project, 1978–1981, Alice, Box 68, SDO\044\0005\3, p. 9.

24 Annegret Mphahlele, interview conducted by Michalina Musielak, email message to Michalina Musielak, 28 March 2023, Bauhaus Lab archives.

25 Ibid.

26 Annegret Mphahlele, German Mphahlele, Gabriele Mohale, Maxwell Mohale, interview conducted by Esther Mbibo

and Michalina Musielak, Johannesburg, South Africa, 4 June 2022, Bauhaus Lab archives.

27 Annegret Mphahlele, interview conducted by Michalina Musielak, email message to Michalina Musielak, 28 March 2023, Bauhaus Lab archives.

28 Ibid.

29 Archiv Demokratischer Sozialismus, inventory: project 'Die Solidarität der DDR und der BRD mit dem südafrikanischen Befreiungskampf', Rosa-Luxemburg-Stiftung, Berlin, 2020-13-39.

30 Gabriele Mohale, interview conducted by Michalina Musielak, email message to Michalina Musielak, 29 March 2023, Bauhaus Lab archives.

31 Lars Jakob Nerg, Wenche Svela, Daryl Sturrock. *Report from African National Congress (SA)'s Vocational Training Centre, Dakawa – Tanzania 1988–1992. From Practical Skills to Trade Education, 16 June 1992.* University of Fort Hare, ANC Archives, inventory: Director's office. Solomon Mahlangu Freedom College, no.12. Mazimbu Project, 1978–1981, Alice, Box 68, SDO\044\0005\3, p. 11.

32 Annegret Mphahlele, interview conducted by Michalina Musielak, email message to Michalina Musielak, 28 March 2023, Bauhaus Lab archives.

33 Gabriele Mohale, interview conducted by Michalina Musielak, email message to Michalina Musielak, 29 March 2023, Bauhaus Lab archives.

34 Lars Jakob Nerg, Wenche Svela, Daryl Sturrock. *Report from African National Congress (SA)'s Vocational Training Centre, Dakawa – Tanzania 1988–1992. From Practical Skills to Trade Education, 16 June 1992.* University

of Fort Hare, ANC Archives, inventory: Director's office. Solomon Mahlangu Freedom College, no. 12, Mazimbu Project, 1978–1981, Alice, Box 68, SDO\044\0005\3, p. 10.

35 Gabriele Mohale, interview conducted by Michalina Musielak, email message to Michalina Musielak, 29 March 2023, Bauhaus Lab archives.

36 Annegret Mphahlele, interview conducted by Michalina Musielak, email message to Michalina Musielak, 28 March 2023, Bauhaus Lab archives.

37 International Institute of Social History, African Skies Foundation Video Collection, 138, https://access.iisg. amsterdam/universalviewer/#?manifest=https://hdl.handle.net/10622/COLL00549.138?locatt=view:manifest, 2 April 2023.

38 International Institute of Social History, African Skies Foundation Video Collection, 139, https://access.iisg. amsterdam/universalviewer/#?manifest=https://hdl.handle. net/10622/COLL00549.139?locatt=view:manifest, 2 April 2023.

39 Sipho Njobe, interview conducted by Regina Bittner and Michalina Musielak, Johannesburg, South Africa, 4 June 2022, Bauhaus Lab archives.

40 Gabriele Mohale, interview conducted by Michalina Musielak, email message to Michalina Musielak, 29 March 2023, Bauhaus Lab archives.

41 Sipho Njobe, interview conducted by Regina Bittner and Michalina Musielak, Johannesburg, South Africa, 4 June 2022, Bauhaus Lab archives.

42 Lars Jakob Nerg, Wenche Svela, Daryl Sturrock. *Report from African National Congress (SA)'s Vocational Training*

Centre, Dakawa–Tanzania 1988–1992. From Practical Skills to Trade Education, 16 June 1992. University of Fort Hare, ANC Archives, inventory: Director's office. Solomon Mahlangu Freedom College, no. 12, Mazimbu Project, 1978–1981, Alice, Box 68, SDO\044\0005\3, p. 8.

43 Ibid.

44 Sipho Njobe, interview conducted by Regina Bittner and Michalina Musielak, Johannesburg, South Africa, 4 June 2022, Bauhaus Lab archives.

45 Lars Jakob Nerg, Wenche Svela, Daryl Sturrock. *Report from African National Congress (SA)'s Vocational Training Centre, Dakawa–Tanzania 1988–1992. From Practical Skills to Trade Education, 16 June 1992.* University of Fort Hare, ANC Archives, inventory: Director's office. Solomon Mahlangu Freedom College, no. 12, Mazimbu Project, 1978–1981, Alice, Box 68, SDO\044\0005\3, p. 8.

● Bauhaus Taschenbuch 2
Architektur aus der Schuhbox.
Baťas internationale Fabrikstädte

● Bauhaus Taschenbuch 3
Kibbuz und Bauhaus. Pioniere des Kollektivs

● Bauhaus Taschenbuch 5
Das Bauhausgebäude in Dessau
The Bauhaus Building in Dessau

● Bauhaus Taschenbuch 6
Vom Bauhaus nach Palästina.
Chanan Frenkel, Ricarda und Heinz Schwerin

● Bauhaus Taschenbuch 7
Die Siedlung Dessau-Törten 1926 bis 1931

● Bauhaus Taschenbuch 9
Die unsichtbare Bauhausstadt. Eine Spurensuche
in Dessau

● Bauhaus Taschenbuch 11
Junges Design am Bauhaus Dessau

● Bauhaus Taschenbuch 12
Bauhaus Lab 2013. Architecture after Speculation

● Bauhaus Taschenbuch 14
Die Werkbundsiedlung Stuttgart Weissenhof